# Fluid Divinity

## Taylor Talks

Presentation by *BookLeaf Publishing*

Web: www.bookleafpub.com

E-mail: info@bookleafpub.com

ISBN: 9789357441469

First edition 2023

# DEDICATION

It's only right that I dedicate this book to my grandmother, Violet Shaw. She passed away December 9th, 2006 when I was 12 years old, but her booming spirit continues to live on through me. Her birthday was the Fourth of the July and the fireworks she's left in my spirit have not and will never settle. For now and forever, I credit this book to you my love. Thank you for the planting of this seed and allowing me to water it into greatness. This is only the beginning.

# ACKNOWLEDGEMENT

Ashley, you may not be my twin flame, but time only continues to prove that you are my twin spirit. Thank you for inviting me to participate in this challenge with you. This opportunity meant more to me than you may ever know, even though I know that you know. I'm eternally grateful for our friendship, our sisterhood, and your existence.

Kingston, my shining sun. You mean the world to me, and I thank you for facilitating healing me in ways I never thought possible. As I am proud of you, and always want you to be proud of yourself, I also want you to be proud of me too. Every move I make has you in mind and I hope one day you understand how instrumental you have been in this divine shift of my own existence.

She who has yet to be named. Girl the groundbreaking changes you've made for me and you're not even earth-side yet. That alone speaks volumes in itself. I'm forever in gratitude for who you are, who you will be, and all that you represent in this realm and the next. And I know that you'll be proud of me too.

And to The Universe, I asked you to show me the magic, and you've done nothing but ever since. I give my gratitude.

# PREFACE

To begin, I would just like to say that even when themes may repeat themselves, this collection of poems is in no particular order. I initially intended to organize them in a way that they flow together rationally, only to rationalize with myself that thoughts often don't flow in a certain order. They come as they come. Messy, sporadic, at times chaotic or repetitive. The writing in itself is the organization of said thoughts. And that is what I wanted to display. The artistry created through my thoughts. Highlighting that we embody many different things at one time, never only one thing in any given moment. Be it very exquisite or highly explicit (which is a warning because the vibe and content is subject to change instantaneously). So feel free to move about the book as you see fit, as your spirit may be guided to a certain piece, or page, or moment in time over another.

# Disclaimer

You are the most yourself around the people you're closest to, so they hold both the privilege and the burden to experience the very best and the very worst sides of you.

So if I invite you in, I advise you to be careful, as I am more than just my exterior, and I am more than just my best side.

Welcome.

# A Letter To My Child

You don't know who you are yet
But I know who you'll become
The victories you will face
And the triumphs you'll overcome
I see much greatness in your future
Even more than in my own
For this prince awaits a throne
And to God be the glory
For my unborn son

# To My Son

You're so much more than your existence
The greatness inside of you destines you to become
more than just who you are
Because who you are stands for more than just your
reservation on this earth
But rather it speaks volumes to what you can do
Because the things that you will make happen will
represent much more than an action
But rather a key to create a shift on this planet
And a movement to our people

You are much more than a body
Much more than a being
You are a vessel
For peace
For prosperity
For hope
For love
For change
Before you were birthed outside of me
Before you were born inside of me
Before your simple existence
It was God that predestined you to become much
more than they will recognize you to be

My son
For you are a king

# A Call To Recognition

Do we hate ourselves?
We can't all be so pro-black and still use the word
nigga so loosely...
It's as though we don't know our own history. And
please don't fault me, because I am guilty of this too
But with that being said again I ask you, do WE, hate
OURSELVES?
With as many shades of butter pecan, caramel,
mocha, honey, cocoa butter browns there are we still
can't come up with a term of endearment that we
didn't assimilate from the white race that so poorly
thought of our very existence, let alone our
complexion?

I disagree.

And I would say that it's time we do better, my
brothas. And do better my sistas.
For we are, have been, and will always continue to be
royalty.
So stand up and wear your crowns my kings and my
queens, and wear them proudly.
It's time to know your names.

Because you have thrones to claim.

# You Make Me Wanna…

I just wanna touch you without touching you...
Make you come without calling you
Would it be okay if I teased you?
Make fun for me, and you?
I'll make you scream if you want
Even cry if you must
I just want to feel your energy
Hear it call my name
Release your inhibitions
Have them begging to be tamed
Just touch you without touching you
Let your aura feel mine
Want me till you can't anymore
Because now your soul needs mine

# PTSD

Flashbacks reminding you how you'll never get
it like that again
How another woman could never touch you
again
Taste you again
Fulfill you again
The way I
Once did
Bold
Vivid
Lucid dreams of ecstasy
Yet a nightmare that you'll never see me again
Forever longing for me
Deeply hurting, deeply craving
Always missing, and never recovering
My name will stay on your lips for eternity

# I Just Wanna Fuck

I'm not in the mood for makin love.
We can make love later…
But for now just put it on me
I want my back broke.
And my hair pulled.
Choke me.
Bite me.
Please me.
Fuck me.
Make this pussy cry, and put some tears in my eyes.
Do me good.
Do me right.
The kinda dick that keeps me up at night.
I wanna moan.
I wanna scream.
Do what you have to to make this pussy cream.
Don't let me run.
Make me take it.
Slow strokes.
And deep strokes.
The orgasm where I can't fake it.
Leave me shakin.
Talk to me nice.
Talk to me dirty.
I need it now, I don't mean later.
Pronto and filthy.

# Help Wanted Sign

I'm in need of being adored. Worshipped. And
cared for.
My divine feminine energy is longing to be
longed for.
In search of a satiable appetite that only we can
satisfy.
For long days and on long nights, open you up
and let us live inside.
Allow me to help you, the way you need to be
helped.
Help you, heal you, touch you and make sure it's
felt.
I want you to need me, on your heart and on
your breath there I am
Touch you the way you need to be touched, in a
way that no one else can.

# She

He say he hit the jackpot when he found me
Say he get higher than a crack pipe when he
around me
Your mother sister lover and friend
When I come around time stands still and there
is no end
To the joy I bring
The song his heart sings
Sounds like a melody of peace ecstasy and
divine energy
That water go deep like the depths of the sea
Willing to drown and take one for the team
His spirit team says risk it all for this one
Tell em send the check it's a wrap wit this one
Got lost in love and don't wanna be found
She got that butter love, that cocoa brown
Another she you will never find, a treasure hunt
seek and find
Who is she?
They all wanna know
It's that love and light, that goddess glow
Who is she?
You may never know
Just call for Oshun and watch that water flow

# To My Children

I'll always love you, even when it's hard
I'll always love you, even when I'm mad
Your hard times are my hard times
We're in this together
Snow, rain, or shine
No matter the weather
The "terrible twos" and "even worse threes" will
never be either to me
Tough, that it is
And trying without a doubt
But you're just life for me
All that you do, I experience it with you
When it's hard for me, it's hard for you too
Just know that I see you
And I appreciate you a lot
I love you the most
Even if you feel I do not
Always remember, and never forget
You are mommy's blessing
A gift from the divine
You chose me, not the other way around
For that I am grateful
For deeming me fit
To experience this journey by the pathway
you've lit

# Spirit Has Spoken

I am a light to the world. To others and to myself. I am giving. The gift of insight. The gift of intuition. The gift of light. "Let there be light," said God. And then there was me. Within the darkness I shine, for there is not one without the other. In the darkness I thrive. Illuminating each pathway before me. Amongst the depths I rise. Anyone looking close enough will rise along with me. I am light. I am sound. I am air. I am fire. I am spirit. I embody the divine, masculine just as much as feminine. I bring harmony to each side, bringing along clarity. Definition. I am heart. I am breath. I am water. I flow effortlessly with my frequency. I am precious. I am unique. I am jewelry. I am poetry. I am the most of Thee. I am that I am. That I am. I am earth. I am north east south and west. I am realization. I am fact. I am thought. I am dream. I am manifestation. I am mother. I am giver of life. I am fruition. I am existence. I am soul. I am. That I am.

# Identity Crisis

I know you want to live your life, but now you have to live your life with them too. While there may be parts of your life that you can live without them, there are no parts of their life that they can live without you. You are the facilitator of their entire existence. To live for them, means to live with them.

- A Mother

# Spirit Mathematics

I am the one
And that one is she
She is me
And she is we
Now that's me x three
And that makes we too

I am she
And she is me
She is we
And that's me x three
And we makes us
And us is four
Then plus my spirit guides
And five makes it just… right
Add in the archangels and the orisha
Now I'm six and then seven
Mix in the soul tribe and now we're at eight
Then comes love
Then abundance
At number ten, never late

Now what am I?
Divine in every way
Highly backed and protected
I do what God say

So now who is we?
I is we
And who is we?
We is God
Moving in kingdom authority
Never getting lost in what they say is the
majority
Follow the numbers and follow the way
When you listen the spirit speaks
And will lead you all the way

# Matrix

Standing on the outside looking in, observing
my neighborhood then and now… the shift of
the world is evident
Where peace once was now lies common
disruption
Familiarity lies in the commonness creating a
foundation of chaos as a stabilizing element…
and now the world lives amongst the frequency
of chaos, on which they now must live to
survive
Unlearning to relearn is a means of proper
survival, because I must live where MY
frequency thrives
I rather not lay low and die, but instead vibrate
high
In order to do more than just survive

# Rising Flow

I am so ENTERPRISING.
Anything I seek to create is already made.
The ideas flow in like water, electrified by
action, and purified with intention.
I am a master manifestor, and my ideas are like
the power of real gold.
Too big to hold, and far too precious to be sold.
I bestow upon them the greatness that comes
from within, from the source of infinity.
Within the source of infinite creation.
I vow my greatness freak the world, in a way
they weren't ready to be touched.
Is that too much?
Because I will never do too little.
Because with hands like these they are bound to
wanna fuck…
With my energy. With my ability.
But for me? It is the agility
The swiftness of creation, unmatched and
unstoppable
Unlimited. And unfathomable
Anything I think comes into fruition
Should I put this magic pen on this paper, in the
blink of an eye becomes creation
I am enterprising

I am resourceful
I am the greatest thing to happen to myself
And to them too if they're fortunate enough to
be of witness to myself
Watch me work if you are lucky
Watch me build a dream like you've never seen
a dream been built before
Watch as the creation embodies the creator
And see where the magic begins

# The Addiction

They say love is a drug…
But really I think it's pleasure
Once the high wears off now I hate you and I
need another fix from you again
But if I don't fix myself the fix you give will
only always be temporary
Just like the hit from the pipe, the smoke from
the blunt, the love injected from the needle…
Love is unstoppable
But only when it's real
True love is what you wanted to feel
But until you can give it, you will never receive
it
Only when you heal
Can you feel
The real
But instead with the devil you make a deal
Not to heal
But to feel
What you thought was real
Eatin up pleasure like a full course meal
But are you full?
Or are you hungry still…

Because you'll never be satisfied until you've
gotten your real fill
Of love
And that's not a drug
So it's not in these streets
Look deep within beyond the waves of pleasure
and grab tight to the pain
Walk through the rain
Face your shadows
Until you are light again
This is the thrill
The joy of what it means to feel
Love
For real
Is really just to heal

# Edison

When we first met I thought you shined so
bright.

Until I realized it was just my own light
Reflecting off of you
Back to me.

So when I took my light away
I saw that only darkness remained.

But I'm not the flame to your candle.
So I was never meant to stay.

# Psychedelic

Everything is happening all at once.
Quantum shit.
We're suppressed on this dense ass planet so it
can't be seen that time is truly constant.
The past
Present
And future
Are all right NOW.
You can't see that through the earth lens
But I'm grateful for the veil to be lifted
Grateful for the removal of the imaginary lid on
ascension

# Which Way Is Up?

When your life has fallen down, how do you
pick it up?
When your head is underwater, how do you get
up?
When you're six feet under, how do you stand
up?
When you're only going down, which way is
up?

I've lost myself in the depths of me
Truly seeing what I can only portray to be
But I don't even know
Who I really am
Going day by day not giving a damn
"I don't give a fuck", you'll hear me say
When really my heart just doesn't know the way

Because I'm lost in the abyss of the deepest
parts of my soul
Only hoping that I can come out whole

# Headstrong

I wake up and look at him across the room,
laying on the couch
And wonder why he's not laying next to me.
And then I remember that we're mad at each
other...

...oh…

Please let that shit go.
Won't even look you in the eye cause we got too
much pride.
Say "Baby I'm sorry" and let that shit die.
Want nothing more than that body heat
His arms wrapped around me,
My breast beneath his cheek...

But at what cost will you suffer defeat?
Let love triumph, and place pride under your
feet...
It's funny how I'm saying defeat...
Like I've lost a battle
Like I couldn't be beat.

Stuck between my heart and my head

I have to let one proposer and kill the other one
dead.
But when they're both relevant, how do you
choose?
Between your needs and your wants?
Man, this shit is too much, I need to roll up a
blunt...
Take it to the face and smoke these questions
away
But what will that solve?
Cause at the end of the day?
He's still across the room
And we're still mad at each other
In his head I'm a bitch and to me he's a
motherfucker
Speaking only when necessary
Nothing more, probably less
Keeping quiet is really in both our best interest
Cause when words get spoken it's like blows
being thrown
And neither of us wants to come down from our
throne
See?
There goes that pride.
Why's it so hard to be humble?
Like dropping apologies is really a fumble
A technical foul perhaps, more or less

This whole situation is really a mess…

Two people living together but won't even talk
In the back of my mind I'm saying, "Maybe I
should just walk…"
Away from my heart?
And away from my love?
Now tell me how that's rational when we fit like
gloves…

So I guess that's it.
My answer's right there.
It's way past time to stop playing fair.
Nobody can win when you play by these rules.
On the same team but fighting like fools.

If it's not worth walking away, then here I
stay…

And there I lay…
Next to him…
His arms wrapped around me,
And my breast beneath his cheek…

# Songbird

I am like a song.
Directly relate to some, while just there for
others.
With a melody so sweet, but words so intense.
Either you like me...
Or you don't.
But either way, I continue to play to my own
beat.

Singing to hearts.
Speaking to souls.
Emotions as clear as my lyrics
I wear my heart on my sleeve.
I can easily put a smile on your face.
But just as simply bring tears to your eyes.

If you listen to me closely, and deeply...
You'll find that it's not hard for me to become
your favorite song.

9 789357 441469